W9-AVK-120

Bald Eagles

Written and photographed by Lynn M. Stone

Lerner Publications Company • Minneapolis

For Jean Keene

Additional photographs are reproduced through the courtesy of: © Jeffrey Rich, Nature Photography, p. 14, © Tom and Pat Leeson, p. 22; © D. Ellis/Visuals Unlimited, p. 24; © Art Wolfe, p. 26; © Jerry Boucher, p. 37; © Galen Rowell/CORBIS, p. 38.

Copyright ©2004 by Lynn M. Stone

All rights reserved. International copyright secured. No part of this book may be reproduced, stored in a retrieval system, or transmitted in any form or by any means—electronic, mechanical, photocopying, recording, or otherwise—without the prior written permission of Lerner Publications Company, except for the inclusion of brief quotations in an acknowledged review.

Lerner Publications Company
A division of Lerner Publishing Group
241 First Avenue North
Minneapolis, Minnesota 55401 U.S.A.

Website address: www.lernerbooks.com

Library of Congress Cataloging-in-Publication Data

Stone, Lynn M.
   Bald eagles / written and photographed by Lynn M. Stone.
     p.   cm. — (Early bird nature books)
   Includes index.
   Summary: Describes the anatomy, life cycle, and behavior of the bald eagle.
   ISBN: 0–8225–3034–1 (lib. bdg. : alk. paper)
   1. Bald eagle—Juvenile literature. [1. Bald eagle. 2. Eagles.]
I. Title. II. Series.
QL696.F32S85 2004
598.9'43—dc21   2003000885

Manufactured in the United States of America
1 2 3 4 5 6 – JR – 09 08 07 06 05 04

Contents

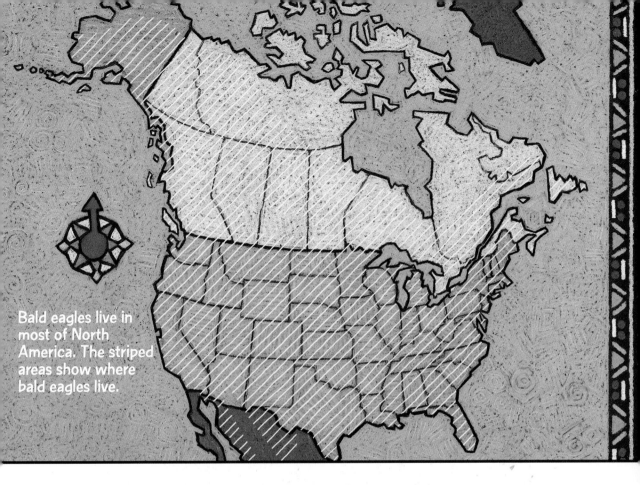

Bald eagles live in most of North America. The striped areas show where bald eagles live.

Be a Word Detective

Can you find these words as you read about the bald eagle's life? Be a detective and try to figure out what they mean. You can turn to the glossary on page 46 for help.

birds of prey	**habitat**	**prey**
DDT	**incubate**	**scavengers**
down	**migrate**	**soaring**
eaglet	**molting**	**talons**
endangered	**perch**	

Chapter 1

The scientific name of the bald eagle is Haliaeetus leucocephalus. Do bald eagles have bald heads?

America's Bird

The bald eagle is the national bird of the United States. Americans chose the bald eagle as the national bird because it is beautiful and strong.

A bald eagle does not have a bald head. But an adult bald eagle has white feathers on its head. The white feathers make it look bald.

Bald eagles are very large birds. Some bald eagles are 3 feet long from beak to tail. That's as tall as a two-year-old child. The biggest bald eagles' wings measure more than 7 feet from tip to tip. That's as long as a couch.

Adult bald eagles weigh about 15 pounds.

Bald eagles live only in North America. They can be found in every state in the United States except Hawaii. Alaska has more bald eagles than any other state. Bald eagles also live in Canada and northern Mexico.

These bald eagles live in Alaska.

Bald eagles often spend time in tall trees.

An animal's home in the wild is called its habitat. The bald eagle's habitat needs to have water, because the eagles often eat fish. Bald eagles usually live near the ocean, rivers, or large lakes. They make their homes in tall trees, on cliffs, or on rocks.

Chapter 2

This bald eagle is eating a fish. What other animals do bald eagles eat?

The Fishing Bird

Bald eagles are birds of prey. Birds of prey are birds who eat other animals. The animals eagles eat are called their prey. Fish is the bald eagle's favorite prey. But bald eagles also hunt seabirds, ducks, geese, rabbits, and other animals.

Bald eagles are excellent hunters. They have amazing eyesight. A bald eagle can spot a fish or a small animal from over 1 mile away.

The bald eagle's sharp eyesight helps it to hunt.

A bald eagle often hunts by soaring. Soaring is flying high in the air. When an eagle soars, it doesn't flap its wings much. As the eagle soars, it looks down to find prey.

This bald eagle is soaring. It is looking for prey below.

Sometimes a bald eagle hunts from a perch. A perch is a place to sit high above the ground. Sitting on its perch, the eagle can see all around it. It can sit and watch for prey.

This bald eagle's perch is a tree branch.

This bald eagle has caught a fish.

To hunt for fish, a bald eagle soars above a
river, lake, or ocean. It looks for fish that are
swimming close to the top of the water. When
a soaring eagle sees a fish, the eagle dives. It
drops quickly through the air toward its prey.

A bald eagle's sharp talons help the eagle to hold its prey.

The eagle slows down just inches above the water. It uses its feet to snatch the fish out of the water. A bald eagle has sharp claws on its toes. The claws are called talons. The talons hold the fish while the eagle carries it.

This bald eagle is protecting its food so it won't be stolen.

The eagle doesn't want other animals to try to steal its food. So it flies to a safe place to eat. An eagle likes to eat on a high perch. The eagle eats in a tree or on a cliff.

A bald eagle has a sharp, hooked beak. The eagle uses its beak to tear its prey into small pieces. The eagle swallows each piece whole. Bald eagles don't chew their food.

Bald eagles are good hunters. But they are scavengers (SCAV-ehn-juhrz), too. Scavengers are animals who find and eat dead animals. They will eat animals that have been killed by cars. They will eat other animals' leftover prey. They will even eat garbage.

This bald eagle is searching for food in a garbage dump.

Chapter 3

Adult bald eagles work together to make nests. Where do bald eagles build their nests?

Nests and Eggs

To begin a family, bald eagles form pairs. A pair is made up of a male bald eagle and a female bald eagle. Pairs of bald eagles often stay together for the rest of their lives.

Each pair of bald eagles builds a nest. Most eagles build their nests high above the ground. Eagles feel safest when they are high up in the air. Then they can see everything around them.

Bald eagles usually build their nests in high places. This nest is in a tall tree.

Some eagles build their nests in tall trees. Others build them on cliffs. Still other bald eagles make their nests on tall rocks that are surrounded by water.

This bald eagle nest is on some tall rocks.

This bald eagle is bringing some grass for its nest.
A big nest may weigh as much as a large car.

The male and the female work together to build their nest. They collect sticks and branches. They weave the sticks and branches to make a nest. The pair fills the nest with grass and weeds to make a soft bed.

A pair of eagles uses the same nest year after year. Each year they add more sticks to the nest. The nest gets bigger and bigger.

Bald eagle eggs are about 2 to 3 inches long. A female eagle usually lays two eggs each year.

When it's time to start a family, the female eagle lays eggs in the nest. Usually she lays one or two eggs. Inside each egg is a baby eagle.

Eagles take turns keeping their eggs warm.

If the eggs become too warm or too cold, the baby eagles inside them will die. So the male and the female incubate (ING-kyuh-bayt) the eggs. They take turns sitting on the eggs. Incubating keeps the eggs at the right temperature. The eagles incubate the eggs for about five weeks. Then the babies hatch out of the eggs.

Chapter 4

Newborn eagles weigh only a few ounces. Which eagle parent hunts for food?

Raising a Family

 Baby eagles are called eaglets. The eaglets are covered with soft, fluffy feathers called down.

This eagle parent is returning to its nest. It may be bringing food for the eaglets.

The eaglets are very hungry. Eaglets grow fast. So they need to eat a lot of food. The father eagle hunts for food to feed the eaglets. While the father eagle hunts, the mother eagle stays in the nest. She keeps the eaglets warm. She also protects them from enemies. Birds such as owls, ravens, gulls, and hawks sometimes try to kill and eat eaglets.

The father returns with food. Then the mother feeds the eaglets. The parents may feed the eaglets as often as eight times each day.

When they are 10 or 12 weeks old, the eaglets are nearly as big as their parents. They have grown long, stiff adult feathers. Soon the eaglets will learn to fly.

A mother eagle feeds an eaglet.

This eaglet is flapping its wings. Flapping helps the wings grow stronger.

An eagle's first flight is hard. The eagle must learn to balance and turn in the air. It must also learn to slow itself down and land safely. Sometimes an eagle crashes into a branch or the ground and is hurt.

The eagle's first flights are short trips from one branch to another. As the eagle practices, it gets better at flying. The eagle begins to fly farther, longer, and faster.

This young bald eagle is protecting its prey from the smaller bird next to it.

Once an eagle has learned to fly, its parents teach it how to hunt. The young eagle learns how to use its good eyesight to spot prey. It also learns how to use its sharp talons to catch food. After a few weeks of learning to hunt, the young bald eagle leaves the nest. It is on its own.

A young bald eagle faces many dangers. It must learn to be a good hunter or it will starve. Many young eagles have a hard time finding food. Some die before they are one year old. But eagles who learn to hunt well may live for many years.

Bald eagles may live to be over 20 years old.

Eagles are always molting. Molting is the process of losing old feathers and growing new ones. A young bald eagle changes color as it grows new feathers. At first, the eagle's feathers are mostly dark brown. But as the young eagle molts, it grows some brown feathers and some white feathers. These feathers make the eagle look spotted.

This young bald eagle has spotted feathers. It will grow new feathers as it gets older.

If this bald eagle lives to be an adult, it will grow white feathers on its head and tail.

Over the years, the eagle continues to molt. It begins to grow feathers that are very dark brown. These feathers look almost black. And it grows white feathers on its head and tail. A bald eagle who has a white head and a white tail is an adult. It is ready to start a family of its own.

Chapter 5

Bald eagles can live in cold places. Where do most bald eagles go in the autumn?

Eagle Travels

Many bald eagles eat mostly fish. But eagles can't catch fish in water that is frozen. In the winter, northern lakes and rivers freeze.

The eagles that live near these lakes and rivers have to migrate. Migrating is traveling between a summer home and a winter home. Most eagles migrate to warmer places in the autumn.

Migrating bald eagles may travel hundreds of miles.

Migrating eagles often travel in large groups. Hundreds of eagles gather in one place. Then they fly together to their winter home.

Migrating bald eagles sometimes stop and rest.

These eagles have arrived at their winter home.

As the eagles fly, they may find a good spot for catching fish. Then they stop and rest for a few days. Finally, the eagles find a place where they will be able to catch food all winter long.

Chapter 6

Bald eagles were once in danger of dying out in most places. What was the main reason bald eagles were in danger?

Eagles in Danger

Not long ago, bald eagles were endangered. Endangered animals are animals that might die out forever.

The main reason bald eagles were endangered was a poison called DDT. People used DDT to kill insects. DDT was sprayed on farm crops and on lawns.

Rain washed some of the DDT off the plants. The DDT went into rivers and lakes. It poisoned plants and tiny animals in the water. Fish ate the poisoned plants and animals. The DDT stayed in the bodies of the fish. When bald eagles and other birds ate the fish, they ate the DDT too.

DDT in rivers and lakes hurts fish. It also hurts eagles who eat the fish.

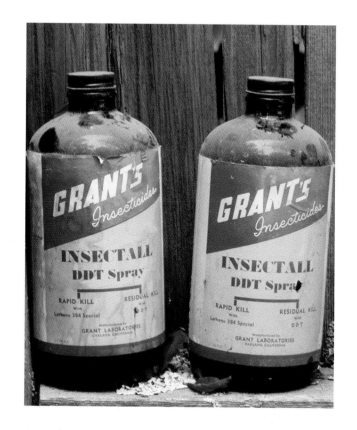

These bottles are full of DDT.

The DDT caused problems. Many female eagles had DDT in their bodies. They laid eggs with weak shells. An egg with a weak shell breaks when the parents incubate it. If an eggshell breaks before the eaglet inside it is ready to hatch, the eaglet dies.

Many eagles laid eggs with weak shells. Many eaglets died before they could hatch.

Few new eaglets were born. The bald eagle was in danger of dying out. Then the United States government made a law. This law made it illegal to use DDT. Over many years, the DDT washed out of rivers and lakes. As time passed, fish no longer had DDT in them. Bald eagles could eat fish without getting DDT in their bodies.

The United States government made laws to protect bald eagles.

Thousands of bald eagles live all over North America.

More and more bald eagles laid healthy eggs. More and more eaglets hatched. The number of bald eagles began to grow.

Bald eagles live in every state in the United States, except Hawaii.

Bald eagles are doing well again. Thousands of bald eagles live in the United States. Many thousands more live in Canada and Mexico.

Do you live near water? Maybe you can see the amazing bald eagle in action. Then you'll understand why it is such a special bird.

The bald eagle's white head and tail make it easy to spot. Have you ever seen a soaring bald eagle?

Have you ever seen a bald eagle up close?

On Sharing a Book

As you know, adults greatly influence a child's attitude toward reading. When a child sees you read, or when you share a book with a child, you're sending a message that reading is important. Show the child that reading a book together is important to you. Find a comfortable, quiet place. Turn off the television and limit other distractions, such as telephone calls.

Be prepared to start slowly. Take turns reading parts of this book. Stop and talk about what you're reading. Talk about the photographs. You may find that much of the shared time is spent discussing just a few pages. This discussion time is valuable for both of you, so don't move through the book too quickly. If the child begins to lose interest, stop reading. Continue sharing the book at another time. When you do pick up the book again, be sure to revisit the parts you have already read. Most importantly, enjoy the book!

Be a Vocabulary Detective

You will find a word list on page 5. Words selected for this list are important to the understanding of the topic of this book. Encourage the child to be a word detective and search for the words as you read the book together. Talk about what the words mean and how they are used in the sentence. Do any of these words have more than one meaning? You will find these words defined in a glossary on page 46.

What about Questions?

Use questions to make sure the child understands the information in this book. Here are some suggestions:

What did this paragraph tell us? What does this picture show? What do you think we'll learn about next? Could bald eagles live in your backyard? Why/Why not? What do bald eagles eat? How do they get their food? How have humans hurt bald eagles? What is your favorite part of the book? Why?

If the child has questions, don't hesitate to respond with questions of your own, such as: What do *you* think? Why? What is it that you don't know? If the child can't remember certain facts, turn to the index.

Introducing the Index

The index is an important learning tool. It helps readers get information quickly without searching throughout the whole book. Turn to the index on page 47. Choose an entry, such as *claws*, and ask the child to use the index to find out how bald eagles use their claws. Repeat this exercise with as many entries as you like. Ask the child to point out the differences between an index and a glossary. (The index helps readers find information quickly, while the glossary tells readers what words mean.)

Where in the World?

Many plants and animals found in the Early Bird Nature Books series live in parts of the world other than the United States. Encourage the child to find the places mentioned in this book on a world map or globe. Take time to talk about climate, terrain, and how you might live in such places.

All the World in Metric!

Although our monetary system is in metric units (based on multiples of 10), the United States is one of the few countries in the world that does not use the metric system of measurement. Here are some conversion activities you and the child can do using a calculator:

WHEN YOU KNOW:	MULTIPLY BY:	TO FIND:
miles	1.609	kilometers
feet	0.3048	meters
inches	2.54	centimeters
gallons	3.785	liters
tons	0.907	metric tons
pounds	0.454	kilograms

Activities

Draw or color a picture of a bald eagle. Be sure to include the place where the eagle lives.

Pretend you're going on a trip to a river or ocean to study bald eagles. How will you get there? What will you take? Who will go with you? What will you see? Write a story about your trip.

Visit a zoo to see bald eagles. How are bald eagles similar to other kinds of birds, and how are they different?

Glossary

birds of prey: birds who eat meat

DDT: a poison that kills insects. DDT makes eagles lay eggs with weak shells.

down: soft, fluffy feathers

eaglet: a baby eagle

endangered: in danger of dying out

habitat: the area where a kind of animal can live and grow

incubate (ING-kyuh-bayt): to sit on eggs and keep them at the right temperature so they will hatch

migrate: to travel between a summer home and a winter home

molting: losing old feathers and growing new ones

perch: a high place where birds sit, rest, and watch for food

prey: animals that are hunted and eaten

scavengers (SCAV-ehn-juhrz): animals who find and eat dead animals

soaring: flying high in the air without working hard

talons: long, sharp claws

Index

Pages listed in **bold** type refer to photographs.

About the Author

Lynn Stone is an outdoor photographer and author who has written more than 400 books for young readers about wildlife and natural history. He has been the author-photographer for several of Lerner's Early Bird Nature Books, including *Gray Wolves, Brown Bears, Cougars, Penguins,* and *Sandhill Cranes.* Mr. Stone enjoys sport fishing and traveling. A former teacher, he lives with his wife and daughter in northern Illinois.